BOOK OF CHILDREN'S PLAYS

FAITH CAPPS

WestBow
PRESS®
A DIVISION OF THOMAS NELSON
& ZONDERVAN

WestBow Press books may be ordered through booksellers or by contacting:

WestBow Press
A Division of Thomas Nelson & Zondervan
1663 Liberty Drive
Bloomington, IN 47403
www.westbowpress.com
1 (866) 928-1240

Because of the dynamic nature of the Internet, any web addresses or links contained in this book may have changed since publication and may no longer be valid. The views expressed in this work are solely those of the author and do not necessarily reflect the views of the publisher, and the publisher hereby disclaims any responsibility for them.

Any people depicted in stock imagery provided by Thinkstock are models, and such images are being used for illustrative purposes only.
Certain stock imagery © Thinkstock.

Scripture taken from the King James Version of the Bible.

ISBN: 978-1-5127-1182-0 (sc)
ISBN: 978-1-5127-1183-7 (e)

Library of Congress Control Number: 2015914579

Print information available on the last page.

WestBow Press rev. date: 10/1/2015

This book is dedicated to my wonderful parents, Rick and Nancy Capps. Their talent to bring the stories of the Bible to life has given me the wings to take flight on this incredible journey. I love you, Dad and Mom!

INTRODUCTION

The purpose of this book is to ultimately help churches, schools, and youth groups with the capacity to provide Godly entertainment, as well as, train individuals with the confidence to perform for future service in the ministry.

These plays are designed to portray ordinary life involving Biblical stories and character lessons that can be applied to every day situations.

Each play includes notes referring to actors and scene changes. Most scene changes include music specials sung by a choir. Because of copyright approval, song suggestions were added to allow the director the use of liberty for individual performances. These may be included or omitted based on the director's discretion. Each play is adaptable to work with any age group and number of class size.

Included in the back of this book are some helpful tips on performing a play. They include some notes and reminders, play, costume, and dress rehearsal notes, as well as, a tentative play practice performance schedule.

The goal through the publication of this book is to aid in the Lord's work, and to help those who seek to see His will accomplished for His glory and honor.

CONTENTS

DEFEATING YOUR GIANTS

CAST

Announcer 1	Coach Saul
Announcer 2	Jonathon
Reporter Ruth	Eliab
Umpire	Abner
Salesperson 1	Samuel
Salesperson 2	David
Salesperson 3	Coach Dagon
Fan 1	Phil Steen
Fan 2	Samson
Fan 3	Gideon
Fan 4	Ehud
Fan 5	
Fan 6	
Fan 7	

Suggested Songs: "God Sees the Heart," "The Star-Spangled Banner," "Take Me Out to the Ball Game," "It's Not by Might"

COSTUMES AND PROPS

Announcer 1—casual attire
Announcer 2—casual attire
Reporter Ruth—suit jacket, Channel 7 badge
Umpire—face/chest protector, hat, broom
Salesperson 1—apron, concession hat
Salesperson 2—apron, concession hat
Salesperson 3—apron, concession hat
(props for salespersons)
bags of popcorn, peanuts, hotdogs, etc.

Fan 1—black and yellow playclothes
Fan 2—black and yellow playclothes
Fan 3—black and yellow playclothes
Fan 4—black and yellow playclothes
Fan 5—black and yellow playclothes
Fan 6—black and yellow playclothes
Fan 7—black and yellow playclothes
(props for fans)
posters, flags, pom-poms, programs, etc.

Coach Saul—team shirt, hat, clipboard
Jonathon—team shirt, hat, glove, cleats
Eliab—team shirt, hat, glove, cleats
Abner—team shirt, hat, glove, cleats
Samuel—team shirt, hat, glove, cleats
David—team shirt, hat, glove, cleats

Coach Dagon—team shirt, hat, clipboard
Phil Steen—team shirt, hat, glove, cleats
Samson—team shirt, hat, glove, cleats
Gideon—team shirt, hat, glove, cleats
Ehud—team shirt, hat, glove, cleats

Catchers—face masks, chest/knee pads, mitts

DEFEATING YOUR GIANTS

ANNOUNCER 1. Well, folks, the first game of the season is finally here, and I hope all of you are just as excited as I am to see how this team plays this year!

ANNOUNCER 2. You said it! There's nothing like showing up to watch a good game of baseball.

ANNOUNCER 1. Sadly, though, the facts about this team show a past of not-so-good statistics. They just can't seem to get over the hurdle of losing. They average more losses than a strainer has holes!

ANNOUNCER 2. True. But what do you expect from a team of midgets? (*Laughs.*)

FAN 1. Let's go, Midgets. Let's go!

SALESPERSON 1. Popcorn! Get your popcorn here! Popcorn! Only one dollar! Get it while it's hot!

FAN 2. Come on, Midgets! You can do it!

REPORTER RUTH. Good morning! This is Ruth, reporting live for Channel 7 News from the home field of the Midgets. Today begins another tough year of competition for this team.

COACH SAUL. All right, team. Get out there and warm up.

JONATHON. Hey, Eliab, you practice some of your pitches while I catch for you.

ELIAB. All right, Jonathon. Just you watch out for my killer curveball!

JONATHON. Well, just make sure you set your sights on the plate and not the dugout.

REPORTER RUTH. Coach Saul, can I get a few comments from you before the game?

COACH SAUL. Sure, but make it snappy. I've got a team to lead.

REPORTER RUTH. Yeah, right. Well, what makes this year different from any other year? Does your team have what it takes to beat the Giants?

COACH SAUL. Well, we've come at this team in previous years, and I don't see why we should go home with a loss today.

REPORTER RUTH.	I've heard the Giants have a new player. His name is Phil Steen. He seems to have the build and know-it-all of a major leaguer.
COACH SAUL.	Well, I've heard it said, but talk is cheap. I stake my claim on the real deal.
REPORTER RUTH.	Well, I'm sure we'll see soon enough. It looks like the Giants have just arrived. Any final words?
COACH SAUL.	Yeah, bring it on, Giants!
ANNOUNCER 1.	There you have it, folks, a quick talk with our beloved Coach Saul. This looks like it is to be the beginning of a great game.
ANNOUNCER 2.	You said it. I can't wait to see the Giants' new player, Phil Steen.
ANNOUNCER 1.	I agree. According to the stat sheet here, it says he was the all-star player for the Titans before he transferred schools to play for the Giants.
ANNOUNCER 2.	You said it. And before that, he was all-star player for the Ogres.
ANNOUNCER 1.	What a guy!
ANNOUNCER 2.	You said it. What a guy!
REPORTER RUTH.	Reporting live from the Midgets' home field, we are about to begin another game of baseball, where the Midgets will take on the Giants. I can feel the excitement in the air as the Midgets prepare to take the field.
COACH SAUL.	All right, Guys. Bring it in. Time to huddle.
JONATHON.	Good job, Eliab. Keep it up, and we may see some strikeouts today.
ELIAB.	Thanks, Jonathon. You're a great catcher.
COACH SAUL.	Okay, team. Listen up. Today we face the Giants. I know they're a tough team, but I believe in each one of you.
ABNER.	Coach, you give us the same speech every time, and it doesn't change the way we play one bit.
COACH SAUL.	You're right, Abner. But you all have it in you. So get out there and play some ball.

(*Play song.*)

SALESPERSON 2.	Hot dogs! Get your hot dogs here! Nice and hot. Only two dollars.
FAN 3.	I can't wait to see the Giants' new player.
FAN 4.	Yeah! I heard he's such a tough player; his cleats are actually railroad spikes.
FAN 5.	Well, I've heard that his pitches sting like lightning. His catcher goes through three gloves a game.
FAN 6.	Can you imagine if he ever hit a batter in the head? He'd probably have to have the ball surgically removed.
FAN 7.	Well, all I know is that the Midgets are in for one tough game.
FANS.	Yeah, I agree.
REPORTER RUTH.	We've heard from the Midgets, now let's see if we can get a few words from the Giants. And here they are!

(*Team comes out and stretches and flexes muscles.*)

SAMUEL.	Would you look at them, they're huge! They must have grown about ten feet since last year.
ABNER.	You're not kidding. Looks like we're toast.
ELIAB.	You mean more like toast *crumbs*!
ABNER.	Exactly.
JONATHON.	C'mon, it's not that bad. We played them last year and lost by only four runs.
SAMUEL.	Yeah, but we don't stand a chance against their new player. Where is he, anyway?
ELIAB.	I think it's that guy coming onto the field now.

(*Mouths drop; heads turn.*)

ABNER.	Unbelievable!
PHIL.	Who's ready to play some ball?
FAN 1.	Look at the size of that guy!
FAN 2.	He must be about nine feet tall!

FAN 3.	This game is over before it's even started.
FAN 4.	Those Midgets are doomed!
ANNOUNCER 1.	Well, folks, the Giants have arrived. Let's get this game started.
ANNOUNCER 2.	You said it. Let the game begin!
ANNOUNCER 1.	Joining us is our field reporter, Ruth. Maybe she can give us a little more insight about the Giants' new player, Phil Steen. Ruth?
REPORTER RUTH.	Yes, thank you. I'm standing here near the Giants' dugout, where they seem to be strategically planning some last-minute decisions. Coach Dagon, do you have a moment for some comments about today's game?
COACH DAGON.	I certainly do. Our team has never lost a game yet. Why, you probably didn't know this, but our team holds the record of ownership of the baseball trophy since it was forged, and we don't plan to lose it today.
REPORTER RUTH.	That's a very bold statement. And what do you have to say about your newest recruit, Phil Steen?
COACH DAGON.	That boy is truly a work of talent. His presence on our team brings such dignity to the Giants' name. He will etch this team's victory in history. From this day forward, future generations will remember—
REPORTER RUTH.	Yes, thank you, Coach Dagon. And now back to the announcers for today's game.
ANNOUNCER 1.	Thank you, Ruth. We'll check in with you a little later. And now, as we begin today's game, we want to remind you to stop by the Snack Shack for all your concession needs.
ANNOUNCER 2.	You said it. They've got everything you need to satisfy that craving, from candy bars to French fries. And don't forget to try their famous, flaming, hot Frito pie. This game's just not the same without eating one of those.
ANNOUNCER 1.	So folks, go on over and check out the Snack Shack for all your snack needs. And now, we will have the singing of the national anthem.

(*Play the national anthem.*)

UMPIRE.	Play ball!
COACH SAUL.	All right! Midgets, get out there, and do what you do best.

ALL.	One, two, three, go Midgets!
ABNER.	Does he really mean what he says? The only thing we're the best at is losing.
GIANTS.	One, two, three, crush 'em!
JONATHON.	C'mon, Eliab! Right over the plate! You can do it. Strike him out!
PHIL.	Yeah, pitcher! Let's see what you've got.
UMPIRE.	Ball one!
PHIL.	C'mon, you chicken! Give me something I can touch.
UMPIRE.	Ball two!
PHIL.	What's wrong with you, pitcher? What a wimp!
UMPIRE.	Ball three!
PHIL.	You gonna take me on a walk today? Maybe you should put a little more speed on that ball. Hey, I know! Move in a little closer.
JONATHON.	Come on, Eliab. Focus. Just do it like we practiced.

(*Phil hits the ball.*)

FAN 6.	It's a hit!
FAN 7.	Look at that ball go!
FAN 1.	It's gonna be a line drive clear to center field.
FAN 2.	And beyond. Why, that ball it's … it's … it's gone! Home run.
FAN 3.	Aww, rats! One run for the Giants.
FAN 4.	Who's up next for the Giants?
FAN 5.	Oh, I think its Samson.
FAN 6.	Yeah, you're right. Look at the way he swings that bat.
SAMSON.	(*Scoffing*) Okay, pitcher, nice and easy. Hey, is that your knees I see knocking together?

JONATHON.	All right, Eliab. You can strike this guy out.
UMPIRE.	Strike one!
JONATHON.	Yeah, good job. Do it again.
UMPIRE.	Strike two!
FAN 7.	All right! Let's go, Midgets!
FAN 1.	Easy out! Easy out!

(*Samson hits the ball.*)

FAN 2.	Oh no, not another hit.
FAN 3.	Oh great. Another home run hit. The Giants have the lead. Two to zero.

(*Samson tips his hat to the crowd.*)

FAN 4.	C'mon, Midgets!

(*Both teams go to the dugout for a timeout.*)

ANNOUNCER 1.	Well, I hate to say this so early in the game, but the Giants seem to be crushing the Midgets.
ANNOUNCER 2.	You said it. Those Midgets could use a little help if they're going to turn this game around.
ANNOUNCER 1.	You know I've always favored the underdog team, and the Midgets are just such a team. If ever they needed a miracle, it would be today.
ANNOUNCER 2.	You said it.
COACH SAUL.	All right, team. This is no time to give up. We've got a game to play, so get back out there, and put your heart into it.
ALL.	One, two, three, go Midgets!
FAN 5.	C'mon, Midgets! Show 'em what you're made of.
FAN 6.	Let's go, Midgets, let's go!

(*Gideon steps up to the plate.*)

UMPIRE.	Strike one!
COACH SAUL.	That's the way to do it.
UMPIRE.	Strike two!
ABNER.	Good job, Eliab! Keep it up!

(*Gideon hits the ball.*)

COACH SAUL.	No, not another hit. I can't believe it.
JONATHON.	Hold him at third. Don't let him score. Good hustle, team.
REPORTER RUTH.	Well folks, this game is not looking so good for our friends, the Midgets. They just can't seem to get ahead, but the game's not over yet. Do the Midgets have what it takes to come back and win this game? I surely hope so.
SALESPERSON 3.	Peanuts! Peanuts! Only one dollar. Get your very own bag of fresh peanuts!
ANNOUNCER 1.	Well, baseball fans, we sure have seen a lot of action from the Giants today. Have you ever seen such athletic ability as that of Phil Steen?
ANNOUNCER 2.	You said it. He certainly has the potential to become the greatest baseball player in the league.
ANNOUNCER 1.	I hate to say this, but the Midgets are no match for such a giant player. One can only hope help is on the way for the Midgets if they are to win this game.

(*Play song.*)

FAN 7.	All right! The Midgets are up to bat.
FAN 1.	C'mon, team! Let's get some points.
FAN 2.	Let's go, Jonathon!
FAN 3.	Put some runs on that scoreboard!

(*Jonathon steps up to the plate.*)

PHIL.	Well, well, well. What do we have here? Oh, it looks like a Midget. Come on, and let me feed you to the birds. (*Laughs.*)

(*Phil pitches, Jonathon swings, and catcher falls into the umpire.*)

UMPIRE.	Strike one!
FAN 4.	Whoa! Did you see that pitch? It nearly knocked the catcher off his feet.
COACH SAUL.	C'mon, Jonathon, you can hit it!
PHIL.	What's the matter? Scared of a little piece of leather?
UMPIRE.	Strike two!
FAN 5.	Aw, man! This does *not* look good.
FAN 6.	Let's go, Midgets, let's go!
PHIL.	Is that all you got? My grandma can hit a baseball better than you can.
UMPIRE.	Strike three! You're out!

(*Jonathon walks back to the dugout.*)

COACH SAUL.	That's all right, son. You did your best.
ANNOUNCER 1.	This does not look good, folks. Jonathon is one of our best players, but he just struck out.
ANNOUNCER 2.	You said it. This team needs some major help.

(*Coaches gather to talk on the field.*)

ANNOUNCER 1.	Look on the field. It looks like a deal is being settled or something. Let's go to our reporter to see what's happening.
REPORTER RUTH.	Listen up! A challenge has just been made. Coach Dagon has just agreed to surrender their baseball trophy if any one player from the Midgets can hit a home run. This is absolutely amazing, folks!
ANNOUNCER 1.	I've never heard of such a thing. To think the Midgets could be within the grasp of the trophy with only one home run.
ANNOUNCER 2.	You said it. This is unbelievable! This could change the future of the Midgets' baseball team.
COACH SAUL.	Whoa, team! Slow down. This challenge is way over our heads. Yeah, it would be nice to win the trophy from the Giants, but it's just not possible. I mean, look at who we are dealing with here!

JONATHON.	But Coach, it's worth a try. There might be a chance we can do it.
SAMUEL.	You've got my hands tied. Where are we going to find someone who can hit a home run?
REPORTER RUTH.	Yes, baseball fans. This challenge is a hard test to take on, but if met, a new chapter could be written in baseball history. Can the Midgets take on the Giants' challenge of hitting a home run?

(*Play song.*)

DAVID.	Hey, Eliab, how's it going? You score any runs yet?
ELIAB.	No, we're losing. Besides, what are you doing here anyway, you little twerp? You're supposed to be at home, raking the leaves.
DAVID.	Dad sent me to bring you some Gatorade and find out how you're doing.
ELIAB.	Well, we're doing terrible, so you can just go back home now. Okay?
DAVID.	Whoa, who's that guy? He's huge!
SAMUEL.	His name is Phil Steen. He plays for the Giants now.
PHIL.	C'mon, you little muffins. Let's get this game going.
DAVID.	What's his problem? Thinks he's so high and mighty.
JONATHON.	The Giants just gave a challenge that anyone who hits a home run for our team will get to claim the baseball trophy.
DAVID.	You're kidding. The trophy?
SAMUEL.	Yep, that's right.
DAVID.	Well, I'd sure like to give it a try. That guy is a bully.
ELIAB.	David, get out of here! He's no match for you. I doubt you even have the muscle to hit the ball.
DAVID.	I do too!
COACH SAUL.	What's going on here? David, what are you doing in the dugout?

JONATHON.	Coach, David wants to face the Giants' challenge. He thinks he can hit the home run that would help our team win the trophy.
COACH SAUL.	Do you think you can? I mean, the Giants are pretty tough ballplayers.
DAVID.	Coach, you *know* I can. Remember all the times I've come to practice and proved my abilities?
COACH SAUL.	Yeah, I remember.
DAVID.	Well, I'm too young to travel with the team to the away games, but I can play on our home field.
COACH SAUL.	That's right, David. Okay, team, let's get David suited up.
ANNOUNCER 1.	I've just heard that the Giants' challenge is about to be taken on by the Midgets. One brave Midget player is going to try to knock one out of the ballpark.
ANNOUNCER 2.	You said it. This place is buzzing with excitement. I wonder who Coach Saul has chosen to be the champion of this game.
ANNOUNCER 1.	I'm on the edge of my seat. There hasn't been this much excitement on the Midgets' home field since … well, never. Let's go to Reporter Ruth and see if she has the latest. Ruth?
REPORTER RUTH.	Yes, the Midgets have indeed found their hitter. It seems as if they have called in one of the extras to take the challenge. His name is David. He may be small, but he's got heart.
FAN 7.	Hey, the Midgets have a new player?
FAN 1.	Do you think he's going to be the winning factor for this team?
FAN 2.	I sure hope so.

(*David tries to walk with his large uniform/hat.*)

COACH SAUL.	Well, David, how does it feel?
DAVID.	I can't move. These gloves are too big. I don't need all this equipment.
SAMUEL.	But you're facing the Giants!
DAVID.	It's okay. I'm not alone. God is with me. And besides, it's time someone teaches that Phil Steen a lesson.

12

COACH SAUL.	Okay, team. Let's do this. One, two, three, go Midgets!
ANNOUNCER 1.	And so, folks, the game has really begun. Can the Midgets put down these Giants once and for all? It doesn't seem possible. But a little part inside of me says there is still a chance.
ANNOUNCER 2.	You said it. This game is not over till it's over. The Midgets are just now getting ready to send out their champion.
PHIL.	C'mon, cupcakes. We don't have all day. Send someone out here, so we can get this over with.
FAN 2.	Can you believe it? That Coach Saul can't be serious!
FAN 3.	Well, I hate to break it to you, but that Midget is our last hope.
FAN 4.	I can't watch this. Tell me when it's over.
ANNOUNCER 1.	And now, folks, coming up to the plate for the Midgets is David. Let's all hold our breath and cross our fingers for this kid.
ANNOUNCER 2.	You said it. I've even got my toes crossed.
PHIL.	What? Is this the best you got? I'll turn this kid into hamburger meat.
EHUD.	Hey Phil! This ain't no Midget. He's a dwarf. (*Laughs.*)
JONATHON.	C'mon, David, you can do it.
UMPIRE.	Strike one!
FANS.	Ooohhh!
ABNER.	Let's go, Midgets! Don't give up.
PHIL.	Aw, sorry about that. That was my granny throw. Better tighten up on that bat, sonny.
COACH SAUL.	Focus, David. Keep your eyes on the ball.
UMPIRE.	Strike two!
FANS.	Ohhh nooo!
ELIAB.	C'mon, David. You can do it.

UMPIRE.	Ball one.
SAMUEL.	Good eye, David, good eye.
UMPIRE.	Ball two.
COACH SAUL.	That's the way, son. Way to watch the ball.
PHIL.	All right, no more Mr. Nice Guy. This time you're going down.
UMPIRE.	Ball three!
ANNOUNCER 1.	Oh, this is too intense for me. The suspense is killing me.
ANNOUNCER 2.	You said it. We're standing at a full count, ladies and gentlemen. This is it! The last throw will determine the outcome of this game.
ANNOUNCER 1.	A hush falls over the field as each player concentrates on this particular moment. These next few moments are critical to the lives of each member of the Midget team.
JONATHON.	David, wait a minute. Remember what Coach taught us about our own strengths?

(*David walks over to the dugout.*)

DAVID.	Yeah. "I can do all things through Christ which strengtheneth me." Philippians 4:13.
JONATHON.	Well, I believe God can help you hit that ball.
DAVID.	You're right. Let's do this.
PHIL.	Hurry it up. We don't have all day.
UMPIRE.	Play ball!
REPORTER RUTH.	Folks, this has been such a great game. I hate to see it all come to an end. David is taking his place at the plate, while Phil is winding up for the pitch and …

(*David hits the ball.*)

FAN 5.	He hit it! He hit it!
FAN 6.	The ball's going up and up and …

FAN 7.	It's gone. He hit a home run.
FANS.	Yes, yes, yes. Hurray! Yippee!
ANNOUNCER 1.	And there you have it, Midget fans. A home run hit as has never been done before on this field. The Midgets win the game!
ANNOUNCER 2.	You said it! The Midgets have beaten the Giants!
ANNOUNCER 1.	But wait! Something drastic has happened on the field. Phil is lying down. He's not getting up. Let's see if our reporter has any information to share. Ruth?
REPORTER RUTH.	Yes, I'm standing here next to some of the Giants' players, and a tragic turn of events has just taken place. It seems that David's winning home run broke his bat, and a piece of it hit Phil in the head, knocking him unconscious. Paramedics are on their way. All I can say is what a game! What a game!
ANNOUNCER 1.	That's the truth! What a game these mighty Midgets have played today.
ANNOUNCER 2.	You said it. What a victory these Midgets have just earned!
ANNOUNCER 1.	Let's get back to our reporter on the field to hear a word from the newest member of the Midgets' team. Ruth?
REPORTER RUTH.	Yes, thank you. I'm standing here with David and the other members of the Midgets' team. David, how was it possible for you to take on such a tremendous team as the Giants? You hit a home run, knocked out Phil Steen, and brought home the baseball trophy. How did you do it?
DAVID.	Well, our coach taught us that only Jesus gives us the strength to do all things. I just obeyed His Word and let God do the rest.
REPORTER RUTH.	Well, young friend that is the best piece of advice I have ever heard. Let's all follow this young man's example of success, and, just maybe, we can defeat some giants of our own.
ANNOUNCER 2.	You said it. What an amazing lesson this has taught all of us today.
ANNOUNCER 1.	Thanks, folks, for joining us here at the Midgets' home field for today's game. I hope you've enjoyed it as much as we have. I'd like to thank each of our sponsors for their support in the broadcasting of this game. Until next time, have a great day!

(*Play song.*)

TO HEAR AN ANGEL SING

CAST

Teacher	Young son
	Father
Older son	Salesclerks
Samuel	Judas
Jacob	Barak
Benjamin	Servant
Reuben	
	Angel 1
Merchant Lady	Angel 2
Rachel	Angel 3
Rebecca	Angel 4
Sarah	Angel 5
Deborah	Angel 6
Lydia	Angel 7
	Angel 8

Optional actors: students, sheep

Suggested Songs: "Bring Them In," "More Precious than Gold," "Amazing Grace," "The Angels Are Singing Again"

COSTUMES AND PROPS

Teacher—church attire

Samuel —robe, belt, headdress, sandals
Jacob—robe, belt, headdress, sandals
Benjamin—robe, belt, headdress, shoeless
Reuben—robe, belt, headdress, shoeless

Merchant Lady—robe, sandals, headdress
Rachel—robe, sandals, headdress
Rebecca—robe, sandals, headdress
Sarah—robe, sandals
Deborah—robe, sandals, headdress
Lydia—robe, sandals, headdress

Optional actors: students, sheep

Young son—robe, vest
Older son—robe, belt
Father— robe, belt, headdress
Salesclerks—robes, belts

Judas—robe, vest, rolled-up sleeves
Barak—robe, vest, rolled-up sleeves
Servant—robe, belt, sandals, headdress

Angel 1—white robe, halo
Angel 2—white robe, halo
Angel 3—white robe, halo
Angel 4—white robe, halo
Angel 5—white robe, halo
Angel 6—white robe, halo
Angel 7—white robe, halo
Angel 8—white robe, halo

TO HEAR AN ANGEL SING

TEACHER.   All right class, settle down. Today in Sunday school we're going to talk about things that are lost. The stories we will learn about today illustrate the joy of finding what was lost. Our story begins in Luke 15. There once was a shepherd who had a hundred sheep.

SAMUEL.   Come along, my little flock. It's time to head out to pasture. Jacob, you coming to help today?

JACOB.   No, I'd rather stay home and work inside the stable.

SAMUEL.   Oh, all right. I'll see you later. Come on sheep. Keep moving. Daylight's a-wasting.

TEACHER.   And so the shepherd left with his sheep and traveled to the pasture, where green grass awaited the hungry sheep.

(*Sheep bleating, playing, etc.*)

SAMUEL.   Oh, it's getting late. We had better head home. Hurry up! Come now.

TEACHER.   And so at the end of the day, the shepherd led his flock of sheep home and into the safety of the fold.

SAMUEL.   Okay, okay, settle down. Into the fold with you. There you go now. What's this? It can't be! I'm missing one. Jacob, Jacob!

JACOB.   What? What's wrong?

SAMUEL.   Count the sheep, and see how many you come up with.

JACOB.   Ninety-six, ninety-seven, ninety-eight, ninety-nine. I only see ninety-nine. Don't we have one hundred sheep? We're missing one. What are you going to do?

SAMUEL.   Well, the sun is almost down. I just can't leave one of my sheep in the field. I'm going after it.

JACOB.   But you can't. It will be dark soon, and then it will be too dangerous. Think of all the wild animals and the robbers.

SAMUEL.   That's why I have to go. I have to save my little lamb.

TEACHER.	And with haste, the shepherd left his flock in the care of the other shepherds and went to find his little lost sheep.
SAMUEL.	Now where could the little lost lamb be? Oh, I hope I find him before it is too late! Please, God, please let me find my lost sheep.
TEACHER.	The shepherd searched and searched, and though he grew cold and tired, he kept looking.
SAMUEL.	Oh, how I wish I could find the lost lamb. He must be so frightened wherever he is. Wait, what's that? I think I hear something.
JACOB.	That silly shepherd. He'll never find his lost sheep. What a waste of time.
BENJAMIN.	Yeah, who cares about one little lamb anyway.
RUEBEN.	Hey, you guys. What's that yelling? Sounds like the Sadducees just discovered a cure for leprosy.
JACOB.	Yeah! Pipe down. What's all the noise?
SAMUEL.	Woo-hoo, I found it! I found my lost sheep. He's all right. Let's celebrate. The lost lamb has been found. C'mon, call the next-door neighbors. Let's rejoice.
JACOB.	You mean at this hour you want to have a party?
BENJAMIN.	Hey, I'm ready whenever you guys are to have a party.
SAMUEL.	Yes! Invite all our friends. Invite the whole neighborhood. Let's celebrate, and tell everyone that once our lamb was lost but is found.
TEACHER.	And celebrate they did. And never was there a more glorious celebration than the recovery of that one lost sheep.

(*Play song.*)

TEACHER.	In the next story, we learn about a lady who had ten coins.
MERCHANT LADY.	Thank you for helping me. You are such a faithful servant to me. Now let me see. Here is your wage, one silver coin.
RACHEL.	Oh, thank you. You are so good to me. I shall always try hard to do my best. See you next week.
	I'm so excited. Now I can buy that new dress I've always wanted.

REBECCA.	Hey, where are you going? You're certainly in a hurry.
RACHEL.	You bet I am. I finally have enough money to buy that dress down in the market.
REBECCA.	Which one?
RACHEL.	You know, the dress in the window at Tabitha's Trends. It only costs ten silver coins.
REBECCA.	Really? That's expensive. It must be a pretty nice dress for that price.
RACHEL.	Oh, it is. Come on—you can go shopping with me.
REBECCA.	Sure, let's go.
RACHEL.	First let me stop by the house and get the rest of my savings.
REBECCA.	All right.
RACHEL.	Oh no! It can't be.
REBECCA.	What's wrong?
RACHEL.	I'm missing one coin. This morning when I counted I had nine silver coins. Then the one I earned today makes ten. I must have lost it.
REBECCA.	Let me count. Well, I guess we're not going shopping. You can say good-bye to that dress.
RACHEL.	No, it's not that easy. I know I had ten coins. We're going to search this house till we find it.
REBECCA.	Ah, what do you mean, *we*? I've got better things to do than look for one little coin. Come get me when you're ready to go shopping.
RACHEL.	Oh thanks. What a friend. See you later.
TEACHER.	And so the lady began to diligently search her home for the lost coin.
RACHEL.	Where could that coin have gone? I know I had it this morning.

(*Rachel looks around the house.*)

Please, God, please let me find that lost coin. You know how long I've been saving to buy a new dress. Wait, what's that? Could it be? Hallelujah! I found it.

SARAH.	Hey, what's all the yelling about in here?
RACHEL.	You'll never guess.
DEBORAH.	What, you won the Galilean Sweepstakes?
RACHEL.	No. I found my lost coin. I had ten silver coins and lost one. I just found the missing coin.
LYDIA.	Whoop-de-do. One little coin.
RACHEL.	One little coin? Why this is more important to me than anything in the world! If you only knew the value of this one little coin.
REBECCA.	Well, I guess I can see what you mean. Want to go get the dress now?
RACHEL.	What, on a joyous occasion like this? No way. I want to invite my friends over and have a time of celebrating first. C'mon, I'll let you help me get everything ready.
REBECCA.	Oh, all right. Let's go.
TEACHER.	And so the lady invited all her friends to come share in her happiness over finding the lost coin.

(*Play song.*)

TEACHER.	The last story we learn about today is about a lost son. There once was a father with two sons. One day at mealtime, the youngest son brought up an interesting topic for discussion.
YOUNG SON.	Dad, I've been thinking.
OLDER SON.	Oh no. This could be dangerous.
FATHER.	Hush, son! Let's hear him out.
YOUNG SON.	Well, you know that my birthday is coming up soon, and I was kind of wondering if I could get my inheritance now, instead of later.
OLDER SON.	What? Are you out of your mind?
FATHER.	Well, I don't know. It's never been done before, as far as, I know. I guess you can if that's what you want.

YOUNG SON.	Oh yes. I do, I do, I do.
OLDER SON.	But why would you want all your money now?
YOUNG SON.	Well, here's my plan. Now that I'm getting older, I want to go to the city and start my own business.
FATHER.	Well, that sounds great, but shouldn't you stick around the farm and gain a little more experience before going and starting a new business?
YOUNG SON.	You see, that's just what I need. More experience. By going to the city, I'll be able to learn more valuable skills.
OLDER SON.	Yeah, right. I'll bet you'll learn more skills.
FATHER.	I really wish you would stay here and help out around the place. Why, the crops in the north fields are just about ready to be harvested.
YOUNG SON.	Ahhh, there's no life for me here. I want adventure. I want to go and take my place in the world.
FATHER.	Well, let me think about it, and I'll let you know in the morning.
TEACHER.	So the next day, with a heavy heart, the father sadly divided his possessions and watched his youngest son leave home for the far city.
	On arriving in the city, the youngest son was taken along by every whim and fancy he saw.
SALESCLERKS.	Get your very own edition of this fast-action video game! Come see the best movie ever produced! Ice cream! Ice cream! Get your ice-cold ice cream! Come one; come all to the greatest show on earth! Get your very own silver-lined tunic for only twenty-nine ninety-nine.
JUDAS.	Hey, you must be new in town.
YOUNG SON.	What? How can you tell?
JUDAS.	I can always tell. It's a specialty of mine. Right, guys?
GUYS.	Yeah! (*Laughs.*)
JUDAS.	You need some help?

YOUNG SON.	Sure. I'll need a place to stay for the night.
JUDAS.	Leave it to us. We know just the place.
TEACHER.	So the youngest son made some friends in the city, who turned out to be the wrong kind of friends. Before the youngest son knew it, his sense of discernment had disappeared, along with his wealth.
YOUNG SON.	Wow, that was the best steak I've ever had. You guys sure know the best places to eat around here.
JUDAS.	Yeah, we should go try our hand at the slot machines down at the casino. You seem to have some luck in your favor.
YOUNG SON.	You really think so?
BARAK.	I know so. Remember the time you raked in the dough at Luigi's?
YOUNG SON.	Yeah.
JUDAS.	Well, there ya have it. C'mon guys. I'm going to the casino. Whoever doesn't come is a real loser!
GUYS.	Yeah, let's go. I'm coming. Me too.
TEACHER.	So once again, the youngest son found himself among friends who were only interested in having a good time. He soon realized his wealth had vanished, along with his dreams, and he was forced to beg again on the streets.
YOUNG SON.	Hey, Judas. Hey, guys. Do you think you could give me some money for a meal today?
JUDAS.	What? No way. We're going to the horse races now. Too bad you lost your own money at the tables.
BARAK.	Yeah. Sometimes you win, and sometimes you lose.
YOUNG SON.	C'mon guys, please? You're my friends.
JUDAS.	Sorry, we got to go. We'll miss the first race. See ya around.
FRIENDS.	(*Laughs.*)
TEACHER.	The youngest son did his best to make ends meet, until the famine hit the land. The economy changed, and jobs were hard to find. He finally found a job,

working for a farmer who owned some pigs. Every day his duty was to slop the pigs.

YOUNG SON.   Here, pigs. Come get your dinner. Oh gross. This stuff stinks. Eww, it got on my shoes. Pigs have got to be the most disgusting animals ever created.

TEACHER.   As the days went on, the youngest son became more desperate. No one gave him food, his clothes and shoes became shabby, and he became very hungry.

YOUNG SON.   I'm starving. I wonder what there is to feed the pigs today. Hey, there's a piece of stale cornbread. It looks a little soggy, but still …

TEACHER.   The more the younger son thought about his empty belly, the more decisive he became about eating the swine's food.

YOUNG SON.   No one's around to see me eat this. One bite couldn't hurt.

Yuck! What am I doing? My own dad treats his servants much better than this. I know what I'll do. I'll go back home to my dad and tell him how sorry I am for sinning against him. I'll ask if I can work for him as a servant. Yeah, that's what I'll do.

TEACHER.   So the youngest son headed back home. While he was still a great way off …

OLDER SON.   Father, did you hear about our losses in the stock market? Grain isn't going for the price it did before the famine came.

FATHER.   Yes, son. I know. Have we heard any news on your youngest brother yet?

OLDER SON.   No. Not since the last report we had of him living it up. Probably won't hear from him again. Dad, you ask about him every day, and we still don't hear a word from him.

FATHER.   I know, I know. He's so young and had so much more to learn. Maybe today will be different. I'll go check the road again.

OLDER SON.   You'll be wasting your time. I'm going back out to the wheat fields.

TEACHER.   And while the youngest son was still a long way off, the father saw him and had compassion for him. He ran and greeted his long, lost son.

FATHER.   Oh, you've returned. I knew you would come back. This is wonderful!

YOUNG SON.	Father, wait. There's something I have to tell you. I'm really sorry about all I've done. I've ruined our family's name and am not worthy to be called your son. Please, just let me work in your house as one of your servants.
FATHER.	What? Nonsense. You are my son. You will always be my son. Come now, we have a banquet to get ready for. Servants, go kill the fatted calf and get supper ready. Bring out my best robe. And son, here is my ring. Put these shoes on your feet.
OLDER SON.	What in the world? What is all the music and excitement about? What's going on?
SERVANT.	Your brother has returned. We're going to celebrate his return. Everyone's been invited to the feast.
OLDER SON.	What? After all he's went and done to father and our family's name. I'm not going. You can count me out.
TEACHER.	The older son was angry and refused to go in. The father finally came out and begged the older son to come in and rejoice with the family.
FATHER.	Son, please. Why are you so upset? Your brother has returned.
OLDER SON.	I have worked for you for many years and have never sinned against you or disgraced our family. Now that he has returned, you kill the fatted calf and throw a party for him, who has wasted his inheritance. You never did that for me and my friends.
FATHER.	Son, all that I have is yours. You shall ever be with me. But this is a time to rejoice. Your brother was to me dead and is alive again. He was lost and is found. Come; let us be happy this day for him.
TEACHER.	And so we see through these three stories how much God takes pleasure in finding that which was lost and the joy He receives when one has been found.

(*Play song.*)

ANGEL 1.	Okay, get ready, angels. Another day on earth is about to happen.
ANGEL 2.	Yeah! It's a Sunday, too. I know we'll get a soul today.
ANGEL 3.	You're right. It's our turn to put that old devil in his rightful place.
ANGEL 4.	You said it. What do you think the preacher will speak about today?
ANGEL 2.	Oh, he always preaches about salvation on Sunday mornings.

ANGEL 4.	True.
ANGEL 1.	All right. Quiet down. The service is about to start.
ANGELS.	Okay.
ANGEL 1.	Shields up. Screens on. Activate protection now!
ANGEL 3.	What do you think about that guy on aisle three?
ANGEL 4.	You mean the one with all the tattoos?
ANGEL 3.	Yep! He's the one. Never seen him darken the doors of a church before.
ANGEL 4.	Let's focus on him, then. Keep all distractions to a minimum. We want him to get the message.
ANGEL 3.	Roger that.
ANGEL 1.	Keep watching, guys. We're only just getting through the intro. This is when the battle starts.
ANGEL 4.	Ten-four.
ANGEL 3.	What's that?
ANGEL 4.	Oh, I don't know. Heard a cop use it one night when I was on traffic duty.
ANGEL 3.	Great. It probably means ten donuts after four. (*Laughs.*)
ANGEL 4.	Yeah, especially the cop that patrols the street next to Donut King. (*Laughs.*)
ANGEL 2.	Hey, focus you two. If we want a win, we've got to do our part. Besides, this is a tough crowd today.
ANGEL 3.	Sorry. You're right. Let's turn on the conviction.
ANGEL 4.	Right, keep it coming.
ANGEL 1.	Listen up. We're coming down to the end. Those demons are really fighting for this one. We can't let them win.
ANGEL 2.	You said it. If ever we needed a miracle, it would be now.
ANGEL 5.	Hey, you guys, look at that!

ANGEL 6.	Is that the Holy Spirit?
ANGEL 7.	It is! He just sat down in aisle three.
ANGEL 2.	He's probably speaking to the guy's heart!
ANGEL 4.	I know. Look at his eyes. They're not so hard anymore.
ANGEL 8.	He's getting restless.
ANGEL 3.	We may get some tears.
ANGEL 1.	All right, everyone get ready. The invitation is about to begin. This is when the moment gets critical.
ANGEL 2.	I've got full power.
ANGELS.	Over here. Here. Here.
ANGEL 1.	Good. Now steady, steady.
ANGEL 2.	I can't believe it.
ANGEL 3.	He's actually doing what the Holy Spirit said. He's going forward.
ANGEL 4.	Well, I never. He's going to speak with the assistant pastor.
ANGEL 5.	Now he's being led over to the soul-winner's bench.
ANGEL 6.	To be dealt with about salvation.
ANGEL 7.	He's gonna do it. He's gonna do it.
ANGEL 4.	Yippee!
ANGEL 1.	Wait a minute! Don't get your hopes up. This has happened before, and it all comes crashing to a halt.
ANGEL 3.	Yes, but look on the screens. Guess who just walked into the room.
ANGEL 2.	It's Jesus! He just broke the chains of sin that were holding that man in darkness!
ANGEL 3.	Hallelujah! He just received salvation!
ANGEL 4.	You can say that again. Another soul brought from death to life.

ANGEL 2.   Amen! He who once was lost is now found.

ANGEL 3.   Praise the Lord! Jesus always comes at the right time to save the day.

ANGEL 4.   Yeah! One victory for us. One loss for Satan.

ANGEL 5.   All right!

ANGEL 1.   Good job, troops. Mission accomplished. Let's go tell the others the good news.

(*Play song.*)

JUST PUT ON SOME PRAISE

CAST

Mindy	Guard 1
Sierra	Guard 2
Chloe	Magistrate
Bethany	Paul
	Silas
Job	
Bildad	Namaan
Zophar	Mrs. Namaan
Eliphaz	Little Maid
Choir	

Suggested Songs: "Keep Walking with the Lord," "To God Be the Glory," "The Joy of Jesus," "I'm Singing," "With a Song of Praise"

Some parts of this script were adapted from the play "Just Put On Some Praise" by Jeanne Hackett.

COSTUMES AND PROPS

Mindy—casual clothes
Sierra—casual clothes
Chloe—casual clothes
Bethany—casual clothes

Job—robe, belt, headdress, sandals
Bildad—robe, belt, headdress, sandals
Zophar—robe, belt, headdress, sandals
Eliphaz—robe, belt, headdress, sandals

Choir—church attire

Guard 1—armor, helmet, sword, spear
Guard 2—armor, helmet, sword, spear
Magistrate—royal robe, crown,

Paul—ragged robe, belt
Silas—ragged robe, belt

Namaan—uniform, bandages
Mrs. Namaan—robe, sandals
Little Maid—robe, headdress

JUST PUT ON SOME PRAISE

MINDY.	Hey, Sierra, wait for me!
SIERRA.	Oh, Hi, Mindy. (*saddened tone*)
MINDY.	Isn't it a beautiful day? I think fall is my favorite season! The whole world is fantastic!
SIERRA.	Yeah, I guess so. (*dejected*)
MINDY.	What's wrong?
SIERRA.	Oh, nothing. It's just that I haven't been doing so well in the candy sale season this year.
MINDY.	Oh yeah. How much have you sold?
SIERRA.	Well, I've only sold three cases. Everyone keeps turning me down. I just can't seem to sell the rest.
MINDY.	Sierra, I know what you need to help you be the number-one candy seller.
SIERRA.	Yeah, what is it?
MINDY.	You need a little praise! That will fix all your troubles.
SIERRA.	How will a little praise help me sell more candy bars?
MINDY.	It's a secret that I found out a long time ago.
CHLOE.	What's this big secret you guys are talking about?
MINDY.	Here, let me tell you. In Isaiah 61:3 it says, "Give unto them a garment of praise for the spirit of heaviness." Whenever I feel downhearted, I just put on the garment of praise, and all my troubles seem to just go away.
BETHANY.	Really? That's amazing! But how can Sierra put on the "praise garment" to help her sell more candy?
SIERRA.	That's what I'd like to know.

MINDY.   Well, something I do to feel better when times are tough is to think about all the ways God has been good to me.

CHLOE.   That reminds me of someone in the Bible who did just that. His name was Job.

BETHANY.   Oh yeah. I remember our Sunday school teacher telling us about the troubles Job faced. He's a perfect example of someone who was in trouble.

(*Make scene change.*)

BILDAD.   Seven sons, three daughters, seven thousand sheep, three thousand camels, five hundred oxen, five hundred donkeys gone, all gone. What a disaster!

JOB.   Well, the Lord gave, and the Lord can take it all away. I am still going to bless the name of the Lord.

ZOPHAR.   How long are you going to keep talking about that? If you had lived a pure and upright life, surely God would have made you prosperous instead of taking away what you had.

JOB.   Oh, I wish I knew where I could find God. He knows the way that I take.

BILDAD.   God is only closest to them who know Him, but hypocrites and those who forget Him will perish in eternal fires.

JOB.   When God takes me through the fires of trouble, I shall come forth as gold.

ELIPHAZ.   Face it, he who does not know God shall not stand before Him. The light of the wicked shall be put out!

JOB.   I know that my Redeemer lives, and praise be to God, though my body be destroyed, I shall see Him.

(*Play song.*)

CHLOE.   And in all this, Job did not sin with his lips. He just put on some praise and kept trusting in God to care for him.

MINDY.   So one way you can put on the praise garment is by praising God for the good things He has done for you.

SIERRA.   Well, what else can you do to feel better in trouble?

BETHANY.   Glad you asked. Whenever I get in trouble, I think of my favorite song to sing, and after a few songs, I start feeling a lot better.

MINDY.   Great idea! I know the perfect example to illustrate putting on praise. Remember when Paul and Silas were thrown in jail? Well, that's what they did in times of trouble.

SIERRA.   They sang songs and got right out of jail?

CHLOE.   Exactly! If it worked for them when they were in trouble, it will work for us.

(*Make scene change.*)

GUARD 1.   These stupid Jews. Why do they come into our city and cause trouble?

GUARD 2.   They start teaching customs that are not lawful for us Romans.

GUARD 1.   Well, maybe a little beating and some time in jail will teach them a lesson.

           Magistrate Guard, make sure these men do not escape. They must be punished for their crimes. (*Cast prisoners into prison.*)

SILAS.   Paul, are you all right?

PAUL.   Yeah, a little sore. How about you?

SILAS.   Well, this is certainly not the excitement I was expecting on these missions trips.

PAUL.   Yeah, sorry about what happened. God must have a purpose for why we have been put in prison. We just have to trust Him in our trouble.

SILAS.   Remember what Jesus promised to those who were His disciples. He said He would be with them always and never leave them. Jesus is with us right now.

PAUL.   You know what, Silas? You're right. Let's start singing a song.

SILAS.   Right now? In the prison? What about the other prisoners? It's probably midnight by now.

PAUL.   Oh well. They're probably not sleeping any better than we are. And besides, the guards are supposed to be on guard. So let's sing them a duet.

SILAS.   All right. How about "To God Be the Glory"?

PAUL.   Great song! That should help us remember why we are in jail.

(*Earthquake takes place, lights flash on and off, and the guard awakens.*)

GUARD.	What is happening! Oh no! The doors are all open, and the prisoners have escaped. I shall be killed for disobeying orders.
PAUL.	Stop! Don't harm yourself. We are all here!
GUARD.	What? I don't believe it! Sirs, I heard you singing about God. What must I do to be saved?
PAUL.	Believe in the Lord Jesus Christ, and thou shalt be saved, and thy house!
GUARD.	Lord Jesus, I believe! Oh, praise the Lord! Please, Paul and Silas, come to my house! You must tell my family, so that they may believe!
SILAS.	Now this is what I call a mission trip!

(*Play song.*)

BETHANY.	Wow, Paul and Silas had it rough! At least we haven't been beaten and thrown into prison lately!
CHLOE.	Yes, what a testimony they were to all the prisoners! They just put on some praise, took a stand for God at midnight, and look how God was able to get them out of trouble!
SIERRA.	Well, I guess I see what you girls mean. But I still don't see how praise can get me selling more candy.
MINDY.	Look at it this way. We all have troubles. Everyone has bad days. But when you put some praise on top of your troubles, everything turns out all right.
BETHANY.	That's right! Whenever bad things happen to me, I just realize that I'm having a good day. It's the things in the day that are bad.
CHLOE.	Everyone goes through life with a choice to make. They can either see life as a glass half full or half empty. This is the decision one must choose.
BETHANY.	That reminds me of a character in the Bible who made such a choice.
MINDY.	Who are you thinking about?
BETHANY.	A little maid who was captured and taken far from her home and country.
CHLOE.	Oh yeah. I remember that story. The Bible doesn't tell us her name. It just tells us about her situation in Syria.

MINDY. She was taken to Captain Namaan's house to be a servant to his wife. While there, she displayed great courage, even among her troubles.

(*Make scene change.*)

NAMAAN. Little Maid, I want you to serve in our house. Your job will be to help my wife in the house. Do what she tells you to do, and you will be treated with kindness.

LITTLE MAID. Thank you. I shall try to do my best.

MRS. NAAMAN. I didn't expect someone so small, but I guess we shall work with what we have.

BETHANY. As time went on; this little maid proved her ability and showed she could be trusted.

LITTLE MAID. Ma'am, I noticed that Mr. Namaan has a terrible disease. I heard you talk with him about finding a cure. I think I can help you.

MRS. NAAMAN. Why would you want to help us? You have been taken from your home and family, and yet you still want to help us?

LITTLE MAID. If only Mr. Naaman could go to the prophet in Samaria, he would be able to get the help he needs. My God would be able to cure him of his leprosy.

(*Play song.*)

CHLOE. Because of this selfless, little, Israeli maid, one man was saved and went on to worship the Lord as the true God.

SIERRA. Wow! My troubles that were so huge just a little while ago seem so little now! I'm so glad you girls shared the secret of praise with me.

MINDY. You can put on some praise by realizing how good God has been.

BETHANY. You can put on some praise by singing God's praises.

CHLOE. And you can put on some praise by telling others about God's wondrous power.

SIERRA. Thanks for teaching me to just put on some praise! I think I'm ready to get the rest of this candy sold.

(*Play song.*)

A MODERN PILGRIM'S PROGRESS

CAST

Pilgrim/Christian	Evangelist
Friend 1	Friend 2
Bully 1	Gatekeeper/Soul Winner
Bully 2	Mr. Interpreter
Bully 3	Angel 1
Mom	Angel 2
Daughter 1	Angel 3
Daughter 2	Teacher
Boss	Substitute teacher
Servant 1	Students
Servant 2	Kid/Kind Kid
Servant 3	Frank
Kind Lady	Duke
Faithful	Butch
Lemonade seller	Football Captain
Flesh	Snobby girl
Doubt	Nice boy
Pride	
Discouragement	

Suggested Songs: "Walk with the Wise," "Old Rugged Cross," "Help Me Forgive," "Something to Give," "Be Kind and Compassionate," "Faithful in Little Things," "I'm Thankful," "Faithful Men," "He Will Be Exalted"

COSTUMES AND PROPS

Pilgrim/Christian—tattered jeans, worn shirt/suit coat

Friend 1—jeans, playclothes

Bully 1—jeans, play shirt, ball cap, jacket

Bully 2—jeans, play shirt, ball cap, jacket

Bully 3—jeans, play shirt, ball cap, jacket

Mom—dress

Daughter 1—dress

Daughter 2—dress

Boss—jeans, play shirt, ball cap, jacket

Servant 1—church attire

Servant 2—church attire

Servant 3—church attire

Kind lady—nice church attire

Faithful—suit coat

Lemonade seller—playclothes

Flesh—jeans, play shirt, ball cap, jacket

Doubt—jeans, play shirt, ball cap, jacket

Pride—jeans, play shirt, ball cap, jacket

Discouragement—jeans, play shirt, ball cap, jacket

Evangelist—white shirt, black pants

Friend 2—jeans, playclothes

GK/SW—nice church attire

Mr. Interpreter—nice church attire

Angel 1—white robe, halo

Angel 2—white robe, halo

Angel 3—white robe, halo

Teacher—dress

Substitute teacher—dress

Students—casual attire

Kid/Kind Kid—playclothes

Frank—jeans, play shirt, ball cap, jacket

Duke—jeans, play shirt, ball cap, jacket

Butch—jeans, play shirt, ball cap, jacket

Football captain—team sport shirt, jeans

Snobby girl—casual attire

Nice boy—playclothes

A MODERN PILGRIM'S PROGRESS

PILGRIM.   Oh, woe is me. What is to become of me? This burden on my back is more than I can bear.

EVANGELIST.   Weary Pilgrim, what seems to be your trouble?

PILGRIM.   Oh, sir. I am living in the city of Destruction. This load of sin I carry on my back has weighed me down for many, many years. If only there was someone or something I could turn to for help.

EVANGELIST.   I know exactly how you feel.

PILGRIM.   You do?

EVANGELIST.   Yes. Several years ago I, too, carried a burden of sin, until I met the One Who lifted my load and has promised me a home in Celestial City. The King of that city has changed my name from Pilgrim to Evangelist. I have been sent to guide fellow pilgrims to the place where they can be released from their loads.

PILGRIM.   How is that possible? Can I have my load lifted as well?

EVANGELIST.   Yes. First you must travel to the Gate of Life to have your load of sin lifted.

PILGRIM.   How do I get there?

EVANGELIST.   Here's a map that shows the way. Stay on this road until you come to the gate. Knock and the door will be opened unto you.

PILGRIM.   Thank you. I shall begin my journey right away.

EVANGELIST.   Good-bye, Pilgrim.

PILGRIM.   Good-bye, Evangelist.

(*Evangelist leaves, and Pilgrim begins his trip. Two friends join Pilgrim.*)

FRIEND 1.   Hey, Pilgrim! Wait up. Where are you going?

PILGRIM.   Hi, fellas. I'm on my way to the Gate of Life to rid myself of this load. Want to come?

FRIEND 2.	No way. I've heard stories about that place. It is filled with religious fanatics.
PILGRIM.	Well, I don't know about that, but any relief from this load of sin would be better than what the city of Destruction offers.
FRIEND 2.	Suit yourself. I like my life just as it is. I wouldn't want someone to think I was crazy. Good-bye.
FRIEND 1.	Pilgrim, what's this about the Gate of Life?
PILGRIM.	Well, a man named Evangelist gave me this map and told me about a place called the Gate of Life, where a person's heavy load of sin can be taken away.
FRIEND 1.	That sounds like a good place. I think I'll come with you.
PILGRIM.	Okay, let's go!

(*Pilgrim and Friend 1 depart out and return through the side door.*)

PILGRIM.	The map says the trail goes this way.
FRIEND 1.	Is this the map Evangelist gave you?
PILGRIM.	Yes, he said it will lead us right to the Gate of Life.
FRIEND 1.	This road doesn't look very safe.
PILGRIM.	Ahhh, help! What is this?
FRIEND 1.	Quick, swim out!
PILGRIM.	Friend, help me out! I can't get out.
FRIEND 1.	I can barely get out myself. I'm not sure about this journey. I want to go home.
PILGRIM.	Don't just leave me! Please, help!
FRIEND 1.	Sorry, Pilgrim. I can't stay here any longer. You got yourself in, so get yourself out. I'm heading back.
PILGRIM.	Help, please. Someone help me get out of here!
EVANGELIST.	Oh, Pilgrim! Grab hold of this rope.
PILGRIM.	Help! Save me.

EVANGELIST.	On the count of three, I'll pull. One, two, three. Uhhh!
PILGRIM.	Hurray! I'm free. Thank you so much! What is this place?
EVANGELIST.	This is the Pit of Despair. Many pilgrims get caught here. Didn't you read your map?
PILGRIM.	I guess we got so involved in our conversation, we took the wrong turn.
EVANGELIST.	Well, don't give up. Here's the right way to go. This way leads around the Pit of Despair.
PILGRIM.	Thank you for coming at the right time. You really helped me.
EVANGELIST.	You're welcome. Now be careful. Many dangers lie ahead of you. Here's a tract that will help you along the way. When temptation comes, read this. I'll be praying for you.
PILGRIM.	Good-bye, Evangelist. I'll remember what you said. Thank you again.

(*Evangelist leaves.*)

PILGRIM.	I must be getting close. The map shows that the gate is just over the next hill.
BULLY 1.	Well, what do we have here? Looks like a little pilgrim.
BULLY 2.	Hey, he looks kind of tired. Maybe he needs a little help.
BULLY 1.	Here, look at this. This is called a drug. One puff of this will help relieve your pain.
BULLY 2.	Yeah, and here's a little something that will help quench your thirst.
BULLY 3.	Guys, this is my favorite song. Ya gotta listen to this.
BULLY 1.	Here, Pilgrim. Try this stuff. It really helps us.

(*Bullies freeze as Pilgrim recalls Evangelist's warning.*)

EVANGELIST.	"Here's a tract … when temptation comes, read this."
PILGRIM.	Oh, Evangelist gave me this tract. I'd better see what it says. "When sinners entice thee … consent thou not."

(*Bullies unfreeze as Pilgrim rejects them.*)

PILGRIM.   Guys, I don't need this stuff. Thanks anyway.

BULLY 1.   Suit yourself, but you're the one who's missing out.

BULLY 2.   Yeah, what a loser!

BULLY 3.   Come on, guys. Let's meet up with some friends.

(*Play song.*)

PILGRIM.   Well, this must be the gate. What a large gate! Let's see what happens next. Evangelist said to knock, and the door would open. Here goes!

(*Pilgrim knocks, and Gatekeeper lets Pilgrim in.*)

GATEKEEPER.   Hello, weary Pilgrim. My name is Soul Winner, and I am the gatekeeper. Welcome to the Gate of Life. Do you seek salvation?

PILGRIM.   Yes. I'm looking for the One Who will help take this load of sin off my back. I am from the city of Destruction. Evangelist gave me this map and directed me to come to this Gate of Life.

GATEKEEPER.   Well, he has told you the truth. This is where all Pilgrims must travel to receive salvation from their sins. All you must do now is to travel down the Avenue of Conviction. You will come to an old, rugged cross at the end of this avenue. There you will find salvation.

PILGRIM.   Oh, thank you! I want to go there now.

(*As Pilgrim travels down the avenue, his sins are called out, and he realizes his sinful condition.*)

VOICES   All have sinned and come short of the glory of God.
                   There is none righteous, no not one.
                   The wages of sin is death.
                   All we like sheep have gone astray.

PILGRIM.   Oh, what a wretched sinner I am. Please forgive me for what I have done. I'm sorry for all the sins I have committed. May You wash my sins away and offer me Your gift of salvation. In the name of Jesus Christ, Amen.

(*Play song.*)

(*Pilgrim's load is released from his back, and he is free*)

PILGRIM.	What a difference! My burden has been lifted, and I feel such a great change has taken place.
ANGEL 1.	Hallelujah! Welcome, Pilgrim. You have just made the best decision of your life. We are here to help you in your new walk.
ANGEL 2.	Every Pilgrim who accepts salvation is given three gifts to help him on his way to the Celestial City.
ANGEL 3.	The first gift is this birth certificate that states your name has been changed from Pilgrim to Christian.
ANGEL 2.	My gift to you is a new change of clothes. Now that you are a Christian, you ought to look like one.
ANGEL 1.	And last, but definitely not least, is a book from the King that will help to guide you on your way. Follow His Word, and you will be directed in the right way.
CHRISTIAN.	Thank you for the gifts. Now what should I do?
ANGEL 1.	You must go to the house yonder, which belongs to Mr. Interpreter. It is there you will receive instruction for the way of life.
CHRISTIAN.	Thank you, and good-bye.

(*Angels depart; Mr. Interpreter comes from his house.*)

INTERPRETER.	Hello, Christian! Welcome to my house. Please come in. There is much to tell you before you continue on your way. Before you go any further, you must discover the five keys of character that will give you the strength to face the trials that lie ahead of you.
	The first lesson is forgiveness.

(*Interpreter and Christian sit while the lesson is acted out.*)

DAUGHTER 1.	Mom, I'm home from school. I'm going out to play with my friends.
MOM.	No, first you must get your homework and chores done. Your sister has already started on her homework.
DAUGHTER 1.	I want to go now. I can do them later.
MOM.	All right. You may go, but you must be back in one hour for supper.

DAUGHTER 1.	Yes! See ya later.
MOM.	Where is that girl? She should have come in hours ago. I'm really getting worried about her.
DAUGHTER 2.	She sure is going to be in a lot of trouble. She still has to do her chores and homework. Well, I'm going to bed.
MOM.	Wait! I can see her coming. She's home.
DAUGHTER 1.	Mom, I'm so sorry. I had such a fun time and forgot to come when you said. Then it got to be so late, and I didn't want to come home. I'm sorry. Will you forgive me?
MOM.	Oh, honey, yes. Forget about what time it is. You must be starved. Here, sit at the table. Let me warm up your food. Dear, grab those dishes from the china cabinet. And here, we saved the biggest piece of chocolate cake for you.
DAUGHTER 2.	Mom, that's not fair. She gets the best dishes, the biggest piece of cake, and you didn't even scold or punish her.
MOM.	Honey, I've forgiven her because she repented, just like God forgives us when we ask Him. Let's all rejoice in what has happened in her heart. To forgive is to forget.

(*Play song.*)

INTERPRETER.	So the first key you are to obtain is forgiveness. Watch and learn from this next lesson.
BOSS.	Gather around, everyone. Each of you has been given a plant to take care of while I'm away. When I return, I expect a full report of your care of my plants.

(*All exit. Three servants return with plants and produce. Boss returns and checks out the progress.*)

BOSS.	I've returned and want to know how you did.
SERVANT 1.	Sir, I have carefully tended your plant and have produced these tomatoes.
BOSS.	Well done, thou good and faithful servant. Here are your wages. (*Turns to Servant 2.*) And what about your plant?
SERVANT 2.	Sir, I, too, have carefully tended your plant and have produced these flowers.

BOSS.	Well done, thou good and faithful servant. Here are your wages. (*Turns to Servant 3.*) And last but not least, what have you to show me?
SERVANT 3.	Sir, I knew you were a careful and respectful man, so I carefully stored your plant in my garage, and here it is, safe and sound.
BOSS.	But you have nothing of profit to show. Instead, you have been lazy. You shall receive nothing, and your plant shall be given to the first servant.
INTERPRETER.	And that, my friend, is the lesson of stewardship.

(*Play song.*)

(*A bell rings, and bullies surround one kid.*)

FRANK.	Well, look what we have here. Looks like a friendly benefactor. Let me see this lunch ticket.
DUKE.	Hey, Frank. Looks like he wants to buy us lunch.
KID.	Stop. My mom gave me money for that ticket.
BUTCH.	What a mommy's boy. Should have guessed. You need to grow up. (*Laughs.*)
FRANK.	C'mon Butch and Duke, let's teach this kid some manners. (*Laughs.*)
DUKE.	Maybe that'll teach ya to respect your elders. (*Laughs.*)

(*Kid lays on the ground, beaten up. Others walk by and around him.*)

FOOTBALL CAPTAIN.	Wow, what happened to you? I'd help ya up, but I've got to get to a meeting with the football team. Sorry, kid.
SNOBBY GIRL.	Oh, how gross. I hate blood. Why don't you guys ever stay out of trouble?
NICE BOY.	Oh no! Are you hurt bad? Let me help. Oh, your books and papers are all over the place. You're going to miss lunch.
KID.	Oh, it doesn't matter. Those bullies took my lunch ticket, anyway.
NICE BOY.	Well here. You can use my ticket and anything else you need. Just get it, and I'll pay for it later.
KID.	Thanks. You sure are nice to me.

NICE BOY.   Well, that's what friends are for. Now you'd better hurry and get to lunch. See ya around.

(*Play song.*)

INTERPRETER.   That's my favorite lesson. The key of compassion. This next one's just as good.

(*Teacher and kids assemble in a classroom setting.*)

TEACHER.   Class, I am going away on a trip and don't know when I will return. A substitute will take my place. All who faithfully attend every Sunday will be rewarded with a trip to Pleasure Island when I return. See you when I get back.

(*Teacher leaves the room and then returns later.*)

STUDENTS.   Do you think she is really gonna come back this week?

SUBSTITUTE.   Well, she did say it might possibly be this Sunday.

TEACHER.   Hello, is there anyone here? I've come back.

STUDENTS.   Yeah!

TEACHER.   Everyone who was present every Sunday, please stand. All standing will get a free ticket to Pleasure Island. I'm sorry for those of you who were not faithful.

(*Play song.*)

INTERPRETER.   The key of faithfulness is often overlooked. However, it is the one you need the most. The last lesson is thankfulness. Watch closely.

(*Kids sit on curb as a lady approaches them with kindness.*)

KIND LADY.   Hey, kids. What are you doing on a hot day like this? It looks like you need a nice cold drink of lemonade to cool you off.

KIDS.   That would be nice, but we don't have any money.

KIND LADY.   Well, I have just enough for all of you to get a drink.

KID.   Oh goody, goody. Let me have some. See ya!

(*One kid turns around and grabs hold of the Kind Lady.*)

KIND KID.	Excuse me. Thank you for the money for the lemonade. It was very nice of you to do it for us.
KIND LADY.	What a nice thing to say! Were there not others with you? You are the only one who returned to say thank you. You are welcome.

(*Play song.*)

INTERPRETER.	The last key you will receive is thankfulness. Keep these keys and the King's Book with you at all times. They will give you the strength and power to overcome evil as you journey toward Celestial City.
CHRISTIAN.	Thank you. I will remember what you have said.
INTERPRETER.	Good-bye, Christian!
CHRISTIAN.	Good-bye, Mr. Interpreter!

(*Interpreter exits.*)

CHRISTIAN.	Before I go any farther, I better read what the King's Book has to say. There's a bookmark in Proverbs. There's even a highlighted passage at 3:5–6. It reads, "Trust in the Lord with all thine heart and lean not unto thine own understanding."

(*Flesh, Discouragement, Pride, and Doubt enter.*)

FLESH.	Look, it's a Christian. He appears to be alone and easy to defeat.
DISCOURAGEMENT.	My name is Discouragement, and I've come to convince you to give up.
PRIDE.	I'm Pride, and this is Doubt.
FLESH.	I'm Flesh. We're here to get you to change your mind and turn back, unless you'd rather perish.
CHRISTIAN.	But I'm on my way to Celestial City.
DISCOURAGEMENT.	You'll never make it.
DOUBT.	It's too hard, and the road is straight and narrow.
FLESH.	Besides, the journey is not an easy trip. It will take you years to get there.
CHRISTIAN.	It doesn't matter. The King has promised to give me guidance in His Book.

PRIDE.	You don't seem to understand. Unless you surrender, you shall perish.
CHRISTIAN.	Then I shall perish for my King.

(*Battle takes place, and Christian is knocked to the ground.*)

FLESH.	Yes, now we have him!
CHRISTIAN.	Oh, Lord, please deliver me from these temptations. I need your help.
VOICE.	"I can do all things through Christ which strengtheneth me. Philippians 4:13."
CHRISTIAN.	Ha-ya! Take that, you evil foes! With the strength and power of the Lord may you be defeated. Thank you, Lord, for Your deliverance. Now help me to go on.

(*Evil foes depart, and another convert joins Christian.*)

FAITHFUL.	Hey, wait up. Are you on your way to Celestial City?
CHRISTIAN.	Yes, I am. Would you like to come with me?
FAITHFUL.	Yes. I've heard so much about it. My name is Faithful. Let's go!
CHRISTIAN.	All right, Faithful. I'll be glad for your company. We're almost there now.

(*Play song.*)

CHRISTIAN.	Look, Faithful, there it is—Celestial City! Look how beautiful it is. Just like Mr. Interpreter said it would be.
FAITHFUL.	C'mon, let's go.

(*Angels enter.*)

ANGEL 1.	Well done, thou good and faithful servant. Enter thou into the joy of the Lord.
ANGEL 2.	Here are your rewards for all the deeds you have done.
ANGEL 3.	And here are your crowns, which you may place at the throne of the King.
ALL ANGELS.	Welcome, Christian and Faithful, to Celestial City.

(*Play song.*)

ARE YOU READY

CAST

Mama	Groom
Fluffie	Virgin 1 (foolish)
Muffie	Virgin 2 (wise)
Buffie	Virgin 3 (wise)
Willie	Virgin 4 (wise)
Leper 1	Virgin 5 (foolish)
Leper 2	Virgin 6 (foolish)
Leper 3	Virgin 7 (foolish)
Leper 4	Virgin 8 (foolish)
Leper 5	Virgin 9 (wise)
Leper 6	Virgin 10 (wise)
Leper 7	Herald
Leper 8	Servant
Leper 9	Passerby
Leper 10	Jesus

Suggested songs: "Somebody Loves Me," "Obedience," "I Know," "I'm Getting Ready," "Nothing but the Blood," "Are You Ready?"

Some parts of this script were adapted from the play "Willie The Wabbit" by Jeanne Hackett.

COSTUMES AND PROPS

Mama—headband with ears, dress

Fluffie—headband with ears, dress

Muffie—headband with ears, dress

Buffie—headband with ears, dress

Willie—headband with ears, black pants

Leper 1—torn, holey robe, bandages

Leper 2—torn, holey robe, bandages

Leper 3—torn, holey robe, bandages

Leper 4—torn, holey robe, bandages

Leper 5—torn, holey robe, bandages

Leper 6—torn, holey robe, bandages

Leper 7—torn, holey robe, bandages

Leper 8—torn, holey robe, bandages

Leper 9—torn, holey robe, bandages

Leper 10—torn, holey robe, bandages

Groom—robe, headscarf

Virgin 1 (foolish)—black skirt, white shirt, sash

Virgin 2 (wise)—black skirt, white shirt, sash

Virgin 3 (wise)—black skirt, white shirt, sash

Virgin 4 (wise)—black skirt, white shirt, sash

Virgin 5 (foolish)—black skirt, white shirt, sash

Virgin 6 (foolish)—black skirt, white shirt, sash

Virgin 7 (foolish)—black skirt, white shirt, sash

Virgin 8 (foolish)—black skirt, white shirt, sash

Virgin 9 (wise)—black skirt, white shirt, sash

Virgin 10 (wise)—black skirt, white shirt, sash

Herald—white polo shirt, blue pants

Servant—robe, belt

Passerby—white polo shirt, blue pants

Jesus—white robe, blue sash

ARE YOU READY

(*Mama Rabbit enters, dusts her furniture and is obviously reflecting on her children. The three girl rabbits enter. They are cheerful, carrying Bibles, and chattering to each other.*)

FLUFFIE.   Hi, Mom! Gues what! We had a wonderful day in Sunday school today!

MUFFIE.   Yes! We even found out that Professor Hippity-Hop is from Scotland. No wonder he can hop quicker than any rabbit I ever saw! He must have really practiced his hopscotch.

BUFFIE.   He said that he comes from the old country. That's why he has Scotch plaid carpet, Scotch plaid wallpaper, and Scotch plaid decorations all over our classroom!

FLUFFIE.   And he even uses Scotch tape!

MUFFIE.   Mama, guess who else came to our class today.

MAMA.   I don't know. Who?

BUFFIE.   Dr. Jack Rabbit, himself! It was so exciting. When he knocked on the door of our dugout, all us rabbits bounded to attention.

FLUFFIE.   Even Professor Hippity-Hop did, too!

BUFFIE.   My heart was going thumpety-thump-thump-thump.

MUFFIE.   Dr. Rabbit is so wise, Mama. Guess what he told us today? He said something I will never forget.

MAMA.   What did he say, Muffie?

MUFFIE.   He asked us a question to make us think: "How can a rabbit get out of a hairy situation?"

BUFFIE.   (*Laughing.*) Yes, and Bugsy said, "He should get a hare transplant!"

(*All three girls laugh, and Mama smiles.*)

MAMA.   That sounds like Bugsy. But how did Dr. Rabbit say a hare should get out of a hairy situation?

MUFFIE.	He said he should just drop his rabbit's foot, and hop on out of there!
MAMA.	Ah, very good advice as usual. I am so glad you had such a special day today! I've been thinking about you all day long. By the way, Fluffie, where is your brother, Willie?
FLUFFIE.	That is exactly where he is, by the way. I saw him hopping all over everywhere on the way home. He is such a headstrong hare! Mama, I worry about Willie sometimes.
MAMA.	I know hunny-bunny. He is on my heart constantly. He certainly seems to find a way to hop into trouble. I'm glad we have a heavenly Father who loves and cares for us when we are safe—and when we're in trouble.

(Play song.)

WILLIE.	Hi, Mom! I'm home. Did you have a nice morning?
MAMA.	Yes, Willie, I did. I was beginning to worry about you, though. You seem to be getting home a little late today!
WILLIE.	Oh? I was practicing flexing my muscles. See! *(Flexes arm muscles.)* You don't want some hunter to make a rigid rabbit out of me, do you? Besides, I'm getting bigger every day. I'll be strong enough to be out on my own soon.
MAMA.	You are a hardy hare, Willie, but be careful that you don't rush headlong into a rut you can't hop out of!
WILLIE.	I'll be careful, Mama!
MAMA.	Now, is any bunny hungry? I need some helpful hares to make tracks to the garden and come back to the table with two carrots each.
WILLIE.	Carrots again! But Mom, my hair is going to turn orange from so many carrots!
MAMA.	*(Places hands on her hip.)* Willie!
WILLIE.	Yes, ma'am.

(Play song.)

MAMA.	It's time to be thankful. Let's pray. *(All bow heads at the table.)* Enjoy your meal, my little critters! *(All eat.)*
FLUFFIE.	Mmmm-mmm, good!

WILLIE.	Yuk! Mom, my eyesight is excellent, and I am not really hungry anyway!
MAMA.	(*Places hands on hips.*) Do I need to tan your hide, son?
WILLIE.	No, ma'am.
MUFFIE.	Thank you, Mama. That was deee-licious!
MAMA.	You're welcome, Muffie! Now that we are almost finished with dinner, let's have our family devotions. Can someone tell me what we have been learning about this week?
BUFFIE.	I remember. We were learning about being thankful.
MAMA.	That's right. What is thankfulness?
FLUFFIE.	Thankfulness is being grateful and saying so.
MUFFIE.	We should always give thanks for all things unto God.
BUFFIE.	I understand now! No matter which vegetables we get to eat, we should do it with a smile, because our God is good, and He gave us all things!
MAMA.	Excellent, children! Now let's read our story from the devotional book. One day as Jesus and His disciples entered a certain village near Galilee, they saw ten men who were lepers.

(*Scene changes as lepers move to their place.*)

LEPERS.	Unclean, unclean. Stay away, for we are lepers.
LEPER 1.	I only wish there was a cure for our disease.
LEPER 2.	I have heard of One Who can heal our sickness.
LEPER 3.	I have heard of Him, too.
LEPER 4.	You have? Who is this special person who can heal diseases?
LEPER 2.	I think His name is Jesus. Many have been healed by His touch. If we could just get a message to Him, I'm sure He would be willing to come and help us.
LEPER 3.	But who would go for us? Who shall we send to call for His help?
LEPER 1.	Let's call out to those who pass by, and maybe they will know.

LEPERS.	Excuse us; do you know where we can meet with Jesus?
PASSERBY.	Yes. Jesus was just in my city. He healed a boy who was possessed by a demon. He just prayed, placed His hands on the boy, and the spirit left him. What a miracle that was!
LEPER 2.	Please, would you take a message to Jesus, and ask Him to come our way?
PASSERBY.	Don't you know how many people are trying to see Him?
LEPER 1.	But sir, we cannot go to Jesus, for we are unclean. The law states that we are to stay at a distance from anyone. Please will you go for us?
PASSERBY.	Well, I can't make any promises, but I will do what I can.
LEPER 4.	I don't think He wants to help us. Who would want to help a bunch of poor lepers?
LEPER 3.	Look someone is coming this way! Let's see if he knows of Jesus.
LEPER 5.	Sir, do you know of Jesus and where we might find Him?
JESUS.	I am Jesus. What is your request?
LEPER 1.	Sir, we all are unclean. You must not come near us, for we are lepers.
LEPERS 2.	Please, Jesus, Master, have mercy on us!
JESUS.	Sirs, if you want to be cleansed, go and show yourselves unto the priests. They will pronounce you clean from leprosy.
LEPER 4.	Come on, guys. You heard what He said. Let's go!
LEPER 5.	I'm right behind you.

(*All lepers leave, except one.*)

LEPER 6.	Jesus, thank You for what You have done in saving our lives. I know we don't deserve Your kindness. Thank You for what You have done for me. Glory be to God!
JESUS.	Were there not ten of you who were cleansed? Where are the other nine? Only this one has returned to give thanks and glory to God.

DISCIPLE.	Master, this man is a Samaritan. He is not a Jew, yet he has returned to give you thanks.
JESUS.	Rise up and go your way: thy faith hath made thee whole.

(*Scene changes as rabbits regroup for devotions.*)

MAMA.	"Rise up and go your way: thy faith hath made thee whole." So children, you see that only one of the leprous men was thankful enough to return and give thanks to whom it was due.
FLUFFIE.	Mama, did the Samaritan man know that Jesus was the High Priest?
MAMA.	Yes, Fluffie, I think he did. Jesus is our High Priest, Who can set us free from any disease and sin. The leprous man knew Who could forgive him for his sickness and his soul.

(*Play song.*)

MUFFIE.	Mama, could you read another Bible story?
MAMA.	All right, but only one more, because we have another big day tomorrow. Let see, this story is about a wedding.
WILLIE.	Oh no, not another love story. Why can't we hear the story of David and Goliath or Daniel in the lion's den? Those stories are more exciting.
MAMA.	Well, tonight we are going to read this Bible story, and you will get to hear those stories another time. This story is actually a parable that Jesus tells to His disciples about the kingdom of Heaven.

(*Scene changes as ladies gather around the groom.*)

GROOM.	Okay, ladies, gather around, and I will explain my plans for the wedding supper. Of course, all of you are invited to the feast.
VIRGIN 1.	This is so exciting. I remember my sister worked at one of these weddings last year, and she had a really good time.
VIRGIN 2.	I can hardly wait. Just think of all the fun we will have.
VIRGIN 3.	I know. I get to stay up past my bedtime tonight.
GROOM.	Each of you has been given enough money to purchase the supplies you need to perform your tasks. When you hear the cry that will be made on our arrival,

you are to trim your lamps and brighten them for our procession. Then when all the guests have passed, you may follow us to the wedding supper.

VIRGIN 4.	When will you be coming down our street?

GROOM.	That's a good question. I'm not sure how long the ceremony will be, so you may want to purchase extra oil for your lamps. Are there any other questions? (*Waits for an answer.*) Good! See you all tonight!

VIRGIN 1.	How much time do we have before it gets dark?

VIRGIN 2.	I don't know, but we better get to the market to buy our lamps and the extra oil we will need. Want to come?

VIRGIN 3.	Sure, I'll come with you.

VIRGIN 4.	Yeah, me too.

VIRGIN 2.	You girls going to come with us and get your supplies for the wedding procession tonight?

VIRGIN 1.	No, I will get it later. We still have plenty of time, and besides, he gave us more than enough money. I think I will go get something to eat at the street vendor's booth.

VIRGIN 5.	Yeah! He sells really good pita bread. I'll go with you, and we'll get some.

VIRGIN 2.	Well, you had better get prepared some time. Anyone who wants to go to the market, come with me.

VIRGIN 1.	Whatever. She is always trying to be Miss Goody-Goody. We still have a lot of time before the sun goes down. All those who want to get something to eat, come with me.

(*Play song.*)

VIRGIN 2.	Oh, I'm so tired. It must be very late. My lamp has already burned all the oil. I better refill it.

VIRGIN 3.	I'm sure glad we spent a little extra for more oil.

VIRGIN 4.	Hopefully, the groom comes soon.

HERALD.	Make way for the procession. The bridegroom is coming. Go out to meet him. Make way, the bridegroom is coming.

VIRGIN 2.	Girls, wake up. Hurry, we must trim our lamps.
VIRGIN 3.	Look how far down they have burned. We must hurry and make them brighter for his appearance.
VIRGIN 1.	Oh no. Look at my lamp. It is almost empty. Do you have any oil I can use for my lamp?
VIRGIN 5.	No. Oh great, my lamp is almost empty, too. What are we going to do?
VIRGIN 6.	I think the other girls bought some extra oil. Let's see if they will share some with us.
VIRGIN 1.	Hey, do you have any oil we could borrow for our lamps? Our lamps are just about empty. The bridegroom is almost here.
VIRGIN 2.	I'm sorry, but we cannot give you any of our oil.
VIRGIN 5.	What shall we do? Please give us some of your oil.
VIRGIN 1.	Oh, my lamp has just gone out.
VIRGIN 5.	Mine too! Can't you just give us a little to keep the lamps going until they come?
VIRGIN 2.	If we give you some of our oil, there will not be enough for us.
VIRGIN 3.	Why don't you go and buy more oil?
VIRGIN 1.	All right. Come on girls. We better hurry before the bridegroom gets here. We don't want to miss the party.

(*Foolish virgins leave, and wise virgins enter with lamps.*)

VIRGIN 2.	Look, I think I can see him coming.
VIRGIN 3.	Can you hear the music they are playing? It makes me want to start singing right now.
VIRGIN 4.	I hope the other girls hurry, or they will miss everything.
VIRGIN 2.	Well, they should have planned ahead. I wish I could have helped them, but I'm on the last of my supplies now.
HERALD.	Make way for the bridegroom. Behold he cometh.

VIRGIN 2.	Look at all the beautiful clothing. I just love weddings.
VIRGIN 3.	Yeah, I know what you mean. These people are all so happy.
VIRGIN 4.	Look, the groom is waving at us. Oh, he's telling us to get in line behind everyone. Let's go.
VIRGIN 2.	What about the other girls? Shouldn't we wait for them?
VIRGIN 3.	But the bridegroom said we must come with the procession if we are to get in to the party.
VIRGIN 2.	All right, but I sure feel sorry for them. They are going to miss everything.

(*All girls leave, the door is set up, and the other girls enter.*)

VIRGIN 1.	Okay, we're back, and we were able to get a bargain on the oil.
VIRGIN 5.	Yeah, we were able to get it at the midnight special—two for the price of one.
VIRGIN 1.	Hey, where is everyone? It sure is quiet. Do you think the bridegroom has come and gone already?
VIRGIN 5.	I think so. Listen, I can hear music over on the other side of town. They must have started the celebration already. Let's go.

(*The girls go to the house and knock on the door.*)

SERVANT.	May I help you?
VIRGIN 1.	Yes. We are here for the wedding celebration. We had to go buy more oil for our lamps, because we ran out.
SERVANT.	But the master said no one else is allowed to enter. Besides, I do not know who you are. Now, I must close the door.
VIRGIN 5.	Please sir, let us in. We were the ladies who were to light the way for the bridegroom's arrival.
VIRGIN 6.	It was not our faults that we had to go to the store for more oil. We did not know the groom would take so long. Please open the door, and let us in.
SERVANT.	I'm sorry, but the wedding supper has already begun. You are too late. I must go now. Good-bye.

MAMA.   So the servant shut the door and sent the five foolish virgins away, because they were not ready for the bridegroom's appearance.

FLUFFIE.   Mama, the bridegroom in the story is talking about Jesus, right?

MAMA.   Yes, Fluffie. Jesus may come back at any time to receive those who are awaiting His return. Only those who have received Jesus as their personal Savior will enter with Him into Heaven.

(*Play song.*)

MAMA.   Well, my little bunnies, it is time to get ready for bed. I hope you have learned something that will be a help to you in time to come. Now, let's say our prayers. Dear Jesus, we thank You for Your love and care for us this day. Bless Mr. Rabbit as he works tonight and give him safety at his job. Thank You for all You have done for us. In Jesus's name, Amen.

ALL RABBITS.   Good night, Mama.

MAMA.   Good night, little ones, and may you sleep well.

(*All rabbits leave, except for Willie, who begins to dream.*)

WILLIE.   Nooo, don't come. I'm not ready. Nooo, I'm not ready.

VIRGIN 2.   Willie, wake up! Wake up! Jesus is coming. We must prepare for His coming.

WILLIE.   But I'm not ready. I didn't know He would come today.

VIRGIN 3.   You must have been flexing your muscles and didn't prepare for His coming.

WILLIE.   What will I do? Can you show me how to get ready for His coming?

VIRGIN 1.   I'm sorry, but we must begin watching for His coming. I think I can hear the sound of the trumpet now.

WILLIE.   Oh, if only I had listened in Sunday school. I wish there was something that could be done to help me now.

LEPER 1.   You cannot enter into the kingdom of Heaven like you are! Why, you are just as worthless a leper as I used to be. Your life is unclean before God.

LEPER 2.   Yeah, nobody wants you around when your life is so full of self and pride.

WILLIE.   But I don't want to live in sin. I want to get right with God.

VIRGIN 2.   It's too late. He's coming. I can see Him now.

LEPER 3.   Oh, look at how wonderful He is. He's calling out to us to come with Him.

LEPER 1.   Sorry, pal, but it's too late for you.

LEPER 2.   You should have been prepared for His coming.

WILLIE.   No, I'm not ready! Please, please, not yet. I don't want to be left behind. Please don't come yet!

MAMA.   Willie, wake up. What's wrong? I think you are having a bad dream. Wake up!

WILLIE.   Oh, Mama. I dreamed Jesus came back, and I was not ready. Please show me how to be saved. I want to accept Jesus into my heart as my Savior.

MAMA.   All right, Willie. Let's do it right now, so you will be prepared for Jesus's coming.

(*Play song.*)

TIPS AND HELPS FOR PUTTING ON A PLAY

- Notes/Reminders

- Play Notification Note

- Costume/Dress Rehearsal Note

- Play Practice/Performance Schedule

NOTES/REMINDERS

- Make sure you thank everyone who helped in the production of the play.

- A little praise can go a long way.

- Always keep paper and pen handy to jot down notes and reminders during practices.

- Draw pictures of the stage and props. Place characters according to your settings. This will help when directing the placement of actors.

- Delegate as much as you can (makeup artists, costume designers, lights, music, sound, instruments, special effects, etc.), because it will take more pressure off you as the director.

- If using songs for scene changes, type out the words to children's songs rather than using sheet music. Most young children cannot read musical notes and find it easier to learn the words to a song.

- To save money through copies and paper, present actors with just the pages of the script they need to memorize for their roles.

- Instruct actors to speak clearly, loudly, and to always face the audience. Use side actions if speaking to someone behind them.

- Any part of this manuscript may be changed to fit your characters, places of originality, names of characters, etc.

- The number of characters can be reduced or increased to fit your production size. Some characters could be combined, and other parts can be expanded, depending on the number of actors you have to work with.

PLAY · NOTIFICATION NOTES

To Whom It May Concern:

On *Day, Month Date,* students will perform a play. If you could help by working with your student on his or her role, it would be extremely helpful. The goal is to have all parts memorized by *Day, Month Date.* If you have any questions regarding the play, please do not hesitate to ask. Thank you!

Director's Name

COSTUME/DRESS REHEARSAL NOTES

To Whom It May Concern:

We would like to have a dress rehearsal on *Day, Month Date,* for the upcoming play. If possible, please send your student's costume with him or her, where it will be stored safely until the play. If it is something they will need until the play is performed (shoes, coat, and so on), that is understandable. Of course, any suggestions you have would be appreciated.

Name:_____Play Part:_____

Costume:_____

For more information or questions, please contact *Director's Name.* Thank you!

PLAY PRACTICE/PERFORMANCE SCHEDULE

Schedule based on one-hour practices, two days a week.

Week 1   Introduce play and script parts

Week 2   Practice songs/script

Week 3   Read parts/practice songs

Week 4   Read parts/practice songs

Week 5   Work on parts, expression

Week 6   Parts memorized

Week 7   Practice scene rehearsals

Week 8   Practice costume/dress rehearsal

Week 9   Practice prop rehearsal

Week 10   Full practice (parts, dress, props)

Week 11   Play production